FRENCH
Activity Book

SHOPPING

Ros & Colin Pilcher

Everyone should speak a foreign language

Woof
Cat

Meeow
Dog

Primary Language Publications Activity Books

Primary Language Publications have produced a series of language activity books for children aged 7-11 years. Written by primary language teachers, to help you support early language acquisition at home, the series follows the QCA scheme of work for language learning at Key Stage 2.

The books combine simple text and amusing pictures to enable the child to learn from word and picture association. The stickers, certificate, child friendly characters and illustrations make learning a language at home both easy and fun.

This can be further enhanced with the provision of Flash Cards and the Primary Language Publications Language Portfolio, which are available from the publishers. See back cover for details.

There are 10 activity books, all available in French, German, Spanish and Italian, which:

- help the child to learn the core KS2 language vocabulary
- give opportunities for repeated, enjoyable practice
- give the child confidence and satisfaction in their new found skill.

A self teach approach, with complimentary support available on-line from qualified language teachers (www.yourfrenchclub.com), allows even those parents who did not study the language at school to support their child at home. Together with notes and guidance for parents, this will ensure that you give your child the best possible start in learning a foreign language.

Good luck   Bonne Chance
Viel Glück   Buena Suerte   Buona Fortuna

ISBN 0-9547980-1-5
Copyright © by C. & R. Pilcher

All rights reserved. No part of this publication may be reproduced, stored in a retrieval system, or transmitted, in any form or by any means, without prior written permission of the publisher, nor be otherwise circulated in any form of binding or cover other than that in which it is published and without a similar condition being imposed on the subsequent purchaser.

Published in Great Britain 2004

Published by Primary Language Publications, Highfields, Rempstone Road, Belton, Leicestershire, England LE12 9XA. Telephone: 01509 502314.

Printed by The Shepshed Knight Printing Service Limited. Telephone: 01509 502246

JE ME PRÉSENTE ET MES AMIS...

Je muh pray-zon ay maiz am-mee...

Let me introduce myself and my friends...

Salut! Je m'appelle
Laurent

Salut! Je m'appelle
Patrice

Salut! Je m'appelle
Francoise

Bonjour! Je m'appelle
Sophie

ET AUSSI...

ay o-see

and also...

Bonjour! Je m'appelle
Anne-Marie

Bonjour! Je m'appelle
Pierre

Now you are our friends, perhaps you would like to draw a picture yourself and write your name underneath

----

Now to complete this workbook

+where you see:
- a box with the French word below draw the correct picture
- a picture, write the French word on the dotted line underneath
+ you will find new French words at the bottom of the page with their meaning   in English and how to say them in phonetics
+ if you forget a French word just look back through the book
+ there is a full vocabulary list at the front of the book

Je m'appelle	je m'appell	My name is.....
Bonjour	bon-jor	Hello
Salut	sal-loo	Hi there

QUI EST-CE?
key ess
Who is it?

Elle s'appelle

Bonjour

Salut --------------------

Il s'appelle

Bonne chance	bon shons	Good luck
Amusez-vous-bien	am-moo-zay voo be-an	Have fun
Elle s'appelle	ell sap-pel	Her name is....
Il s'appelle	eel sap-pel	His name is....

JE VAIS EN VILLE ET JE VOIS....

je vez on veel ay je vwa
I go to town and I see....

un tabac

le magasin de jouets

la pâtisserie

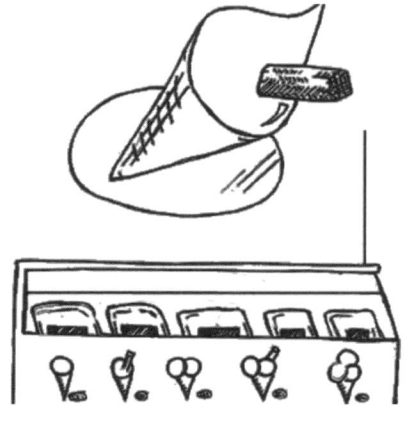

----

un tabac	un tab-bac	newsagents
un glacier	un glass-see-ay	icecream parlour
un supermarché	un soo-per-mar-shay	supermarket
un magasin de jouets	un maga-zan duh joo-ay	toy shop
un marché	un marshay	market
une boulangerie	oon boo-lonj-er-ree	bakers
une pâtisserie	oon pat-tees-er-ee	cake shop

JE VAIS AU SUPERMARCHÉ ET J'ACHÈTE ...

juh vay o soo-per-mar-shay ay ja-shet

I go to the supermarket and I buy....

une limonade

un coca

du pain

un coca	un co-ca	coke
une limonade	oon lee-mon-ad	lemonade
du pain	do pan	bread
du lait	do lay	milk
des carottes	day car-rot	carrots
des oeufs	days erf	eggs
des bananes	day ban-nans	bananas
des petits pois	day petee pwa	peas

7

Sept

ELLE VA AU SUPERMARCHÉ ET ELLE ACHÈTE...

el va o soo-per-mar-shay ay el ashet

She goes to the supermarket and she buys...

du lait

des bananes

----

des carottes

IL VA AU SUPERMARCHÉ ET IL ACHÈTE...

eel va a soo-per-mar-shay ay eel ashet

He goes to the supermarket and he buys...

le gâteau

des tomates

----

un choufleur	un shoo-flur	cauliflower
un gâteau	un gat-tow	cake
une salade	oon salad	lettuce
des raisins	day ra-zan	grapes
des tomates	day tom-at	tomatoes
des fraises	day frez	strawberries

TROUVE LES MOTS

W	E	R	G	H	H	J	E	G	A	M	O	R	F
D	G	S	J	K	A	P	P	L	O	U	E	D	G
A	B	A	N	A	N	E	E	A	F	H	E	P	F
H	J	N	K	K	R	G	T	C	H	I	P	S	S
G	W	D	R	Y	T	F	I	E	J	K	J	J	G
S	F	W	W	Q	M	N	T	I	K	X	C	Z	S
V	R	I	A	D	T	C	S	I	H	L	A	I	T
Z	C	C	V	N	M	O	P	K	H	F	R	I	O
R	T	H	A	F	G	C	O	Z	X	V	O	N	M
H	G	F	D	S	S	A	I	A	A	S	T	T	Y
L	J	H	P	A	I	N	S	L	O	Y	T	G	F
O	E	U	F	X	V	B	D	S	E	W	E	G	H
J	K	L	I	M	O	N	A	D	E	L	S	O	I
D	F	G	E	G	H	J	K	T	Y	R	E	D	B

See if you can help Patrice find these foods in the grid above...

BANANE
COCA
SANDWICH
LIMONADE
LAIT
GLACE

OEUF
CHIPS
PETITS POIS
FROMAGE
CAROTTES
PAIN

LA NOURRITURE

la noo-ree-tyur

Food

La liste d'Anne-Marie

une limonade
des raisins
du lait

La liste de Sophie

du fromage
des bananes
des fraises

La liste de Françoise

une salade
du pain
des tomates

Draw the correct items below the correct trolleys

11

Onze

LA NOURRITURE

la noo-ree-tyur

Food

La liste de Pierre

La liste de Patrice

La liste de Laurent

Write the shopping list for your three new friends
and draw the items in the box below

C'EST COMBIEN?

say com-bee-an
How much?

Au Marché

des raisins	2Euro le kilo
des carottes	0.60Euro le kilo
des bananes	1.20Euro le kilo
des oeufs	2.30Euro les dix
une salade	1.50Euro le demi kilo
des cerises	2.50Euro le demi kilo

---------les dix

---------le demi kilo

---------le kilo

--------------------   --------------------   --------------------

Write the price of the foods below the pictures

au marché	o marshay	at the market
le kilo	luh kee-low	per kilo
le demi kilo	luh dummy-kee-low	per half kilo
les dix	lay dees	for ten

QU'EST CE QUE VOUS DÉSIREZ?

kess kuh voo day-zeer-ray
What would you like?

Moi, je voudrais un kilo
de raisins s'il vous plaît.

Voilà!

Moi, je voudrais un demi kilo de
cerises s'il vous plaît

Voilà!

Moi, je voudrais des oeufs
s'il vous plaît

Voilà!

Moi, je voudrais un demi kilo
de carrottes s'il vous plaît

Voilà!

Moi,

14

Quatorze

je voudrais...	je voo dray...	I would like......
....s'il vous plait	...si voo play	............please
voilà	vwa-la	there you are

JE VAIS AU MAGASIN DE JOUETS ET J'ACHÈTE ...

je vay o maga-zan duh joo-ay ay ja-shet

I go to the toy shop and I buy....

des crayons

un cerf-volant

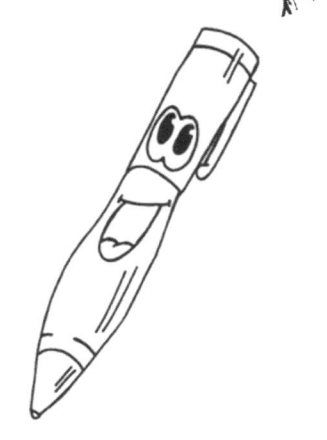

----

un ballon

un cerf-volant	un serf-vol-lon	kite
un livre	un livra	book
un ballon	un bal-lon	ball
un stylo	un stee-lo	pen
un nounours	un noo-noors	teddy
un tambour	un tom-boor	drum
une parapluie	oon para-plwee	umbrella
des crayons	day cray-yons	crayons

15

Quinze

ELLE VA AU MAGASIN DE JOUETS ET ELLE ACHÈTE...

el va o maga-zan duh joo-ay ay el ashet

She goes to the toy shop and she buys...

un livre

un stylo

un nounours

IL VA AU MAGASIN DE JOUETS ET IL ACHÈTE...

eel va a maga-zan duh joo-ay ay eel ashet

He goes to the toy shop and he buys...

un vélo

une voiture

un skate	un skate	skateboard
un vélo	un vay-lo	bike
un train	un tran	train
un bateau	un bat-tow	boat
un avion	un av-vee-on	aeroplane
une voiture	oon vwat-tyor	car

17

Dix-sept

TROUVE LES MOTS

T	E	N	G	H	E	I	U	L	P	A	R	A	P
A	G	O	J	K	A	P	P	L	O	U	E	D	G
M	B	I	N	A	L	I	V	R	E	H	E	P	F
B	J	V	E	L	O	G	T	U	A	E	T	A	B
O	W	A	R	Y	T	F	I	E	J	K	J	J	A
U	F	W	W	Q	M	N	N	I	K	X	C	Z	L
R	R	I	S	T	Y	L	O	V	H	L	A	I	L
S	C	C	V	N	S	O	u	O	H	F	R	I	O
R	T	R	A	K	G	C	N	I	T	R	A	I	N
H	G	F	A	S	S	A	O	T	A	S	T	T	Y
L	J	T	P	Y	I	N	U	U	O	Y	T	G	F
O	E	U	F	X	O	B	R	R	E	W	E	G	H
J	K	L	I	M	O	N	S	E	E	L	S	O	I
C	E	R	F	V	O	L	A	N	T	R	E	D	B

cerfvolant	livre	ballon
nounours	crayons	parapluie
skate	velo	train
bateau	voiture	avion
stylo	tambours	

JE VAIS AU GLACIER ET J'ACHÈTE

je vay o glass-see-ay ay ja-shet
I buy an ice-cream....

une glace au citron

une glace au melon

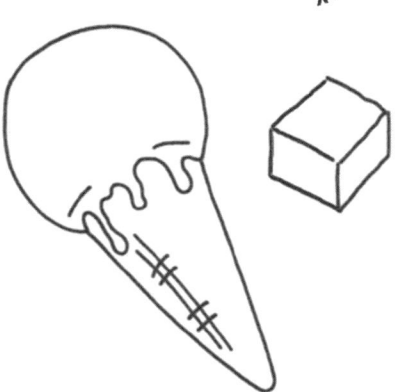

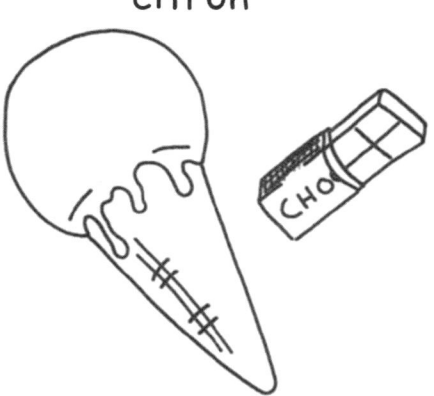

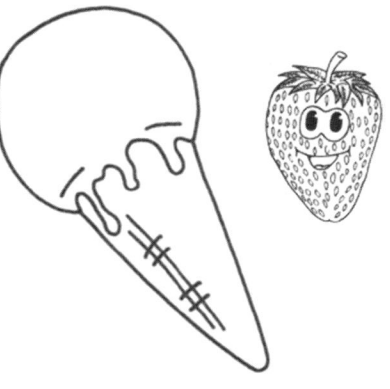

----

une glace à la vanille

une glace au chocolat	oh shoc-o-lat	Chocolate ice cream
une glace au caramel	oh cara mel	Caramel ice cream
une glace au melon	oh meh-lon	Melon ice cream
une glace au citron	oh seetron	Lemon ice cream
une glace à la vanille	a la vanee	Vanilla ice cream
une glace à la fraise	a la frez	Strawberry ice cream

QU'EST CE QUE VOUS DÉSIREZ?

kess kuh voo day-zeer-ray
What would you like?

Moi, je voudrais une glace à la fraise s'il vous plait

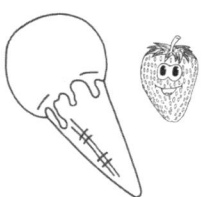

Voilà!

Moi, je voudrais une glace au citron s'il vous plait

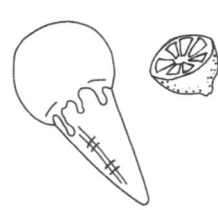

Voilà!

Moi, je voudrais une glace au caramel s'il vous plait

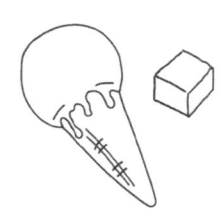

Voilà!

Moi, _____

_____

_____

Je voudrais...   Je voo dray...   I would like......
....s'il vous plait   ...si voo play   ....please

NOUS ALLONS À LA BOULANGERIE ET NOUS ACHETONS...

noos allon ala boo-lonj-er-ree ay noos ash-sh-ton

We go to the bakery and buy...

2 pains au chocolat

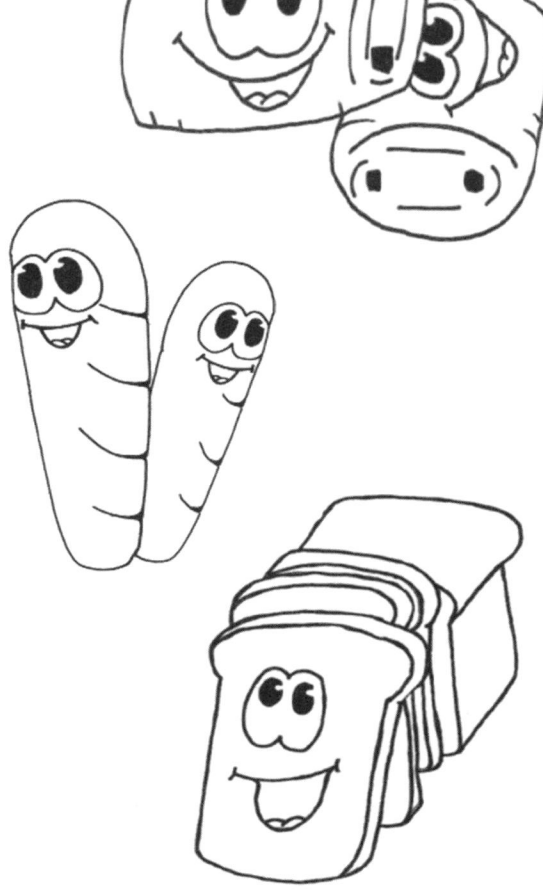

5 baguettes

3 gros pains

4 croissants

Help Monsieur Le Boulanger to complete his orders. Draw the correct number of items. He has done the first one for you.

JE VAIS A LA BOULANGERIE ET J'ACHÈTE...

je vay ala boo-lonj-er-ree ay jashet

I go to the bakers and I buy...

un beignet	0.60Euro
un croissant	0.50Euro
un pain au chocolat	0.70Euro
une baguette	0.40Euro
un gros pain	1Euro
une ficelle	0.90Euro
une réligieuse	1.50Euro
une tarte	1.50Euro

La liste d'Anne-Marie

3 beignets
2 croissants
1 pain au chocolat

La liste de Sophie

une ficelle
4 tartes

ma liste

How much money does Anne Marie spend? ....Euro

How much money does Sophie spend ? ....Euro

Write your own list and workout how much money you spend? ....Euro

NOUS ALLONS À LA PATISSERIE ET NOUS ACHETONS...

noos allon ala pat-tees-er-ree ay noos ash-sh-ton

We go to the cake shop and buy...

  une tranche de la pissaladière

  une tarte aux pommes

  une tarte aux cerises

  une réligieuse

une réligieuse	oon-ray-lee-jee-ers	french cake
une tranche de	oon tronsh duh la	a slice of
une pissaladière	oon pee-sal-lad-dee-air	french pizza
une tarte aux pommes	oon tart o pom	apple tart
une tarte aux cerises	òon tart o ser-rees	cherry tart

ELLE VA AU TABAC ET ELLE ACHÈTE...

el va o tab-bac ay el ashet

She goes to the newsagents and buys...

des bonbons

un cahier

une carte postale

un crayon	un cray-yon	pencil
un journal	un joor-nal	newspaper
un cahier	un cai-yay	exercise book
une timbre	oon tam-bra	stamp
une carte postale	oon cart post-tal	postcard
des bonbons	day bon-bon	sweets

JE VAIS À LA PHARMACIE ET J'ACHÈTE...

je vay ala far-mass-see ay jashet

I go to the chemist and I buy...

des couches

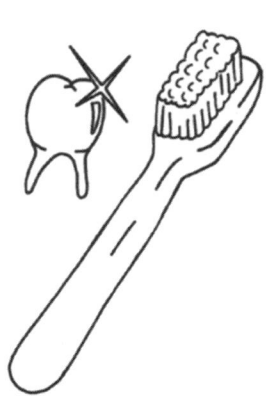

le gel douche

une brosse à cheveux

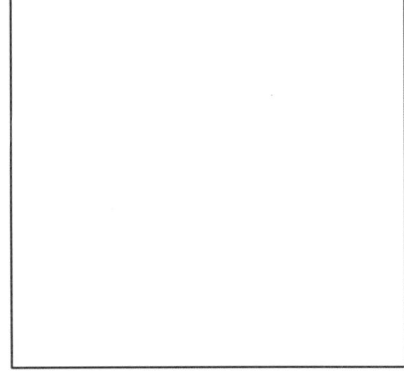

le maquillage

une brosse à dents	oon bross a don	toothbrush
une brosse à cheveux	oon bross a sh-vuh	hairbrush
le parfum	luh par-fam	perfume
le maquillage	luh mac-key-aj	make-up
le gel douche	luh jel doosh	showergel
des couches	day coosh	nappies

25

Vingt-cinq

JE VAIS À LA PHARMACIE ET J'ACHÈTE...

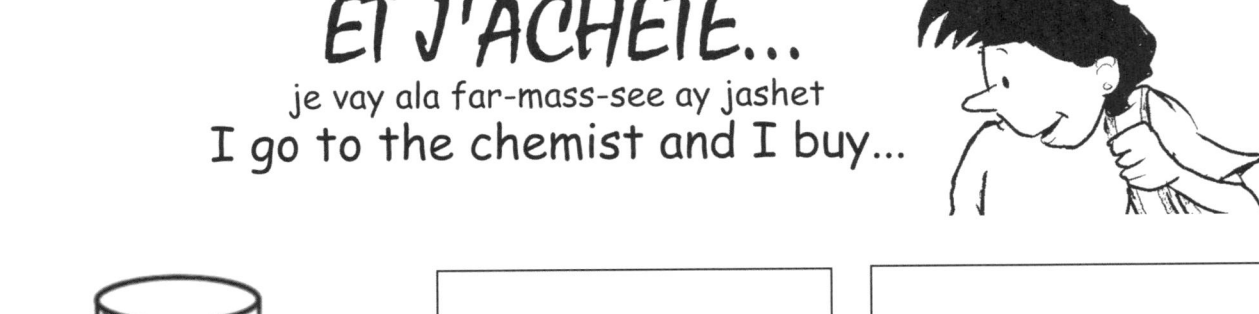

je vay ala far-mass-see ay jashet

I go to the chemist and I buy...

le shampooing

des pastilles

le poudre

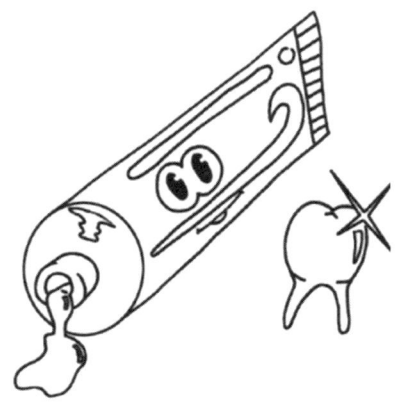

le rouge à lèvres

le shampooing	luh shampooing	shampoo
le poudre de talc	luh poo-dra duh talc	talcum powder
le rouge à lèvres	luh rooj a levra	lipstick
des comprimès	day com-pree-may	tablets
le dentifrice	luh don-tee-freese	toothpaste
des pastilles	day pas-teel	cough drops

JE VAIS À LA PHARMACIE ET J'ACHÈTE...

je vay ala far-mass-see ay jashet

I go to the chemist and I buy...

un biberon

uno brosse à ongles

le lait de magnèsie

un biberon	un bee-be-ron	baby's bottle
le lait de magnèsie	luh lay duh mag-nay-zee	milk of magnesia
le medicament	luh mag dee-ca-mon	medicine
une brosse à ongles	oon-brossa ongla	nail brush
le vernis à ongles	luh ver-nee a ongla	nail varnish
les ciseaux	lay see-zo	scissors

La Pharmacie

There are almost as many chemists in France as there are bakeries. The french are equally passionate about their bread and their health or ill health! The pharmacist is very often the first to diagnose an ailment since the french are more likely to go to the pharmacist than the doctor. But the pharmacist also can be relied upon to confirm if a mushroom is poisonous or if it is good to eat.

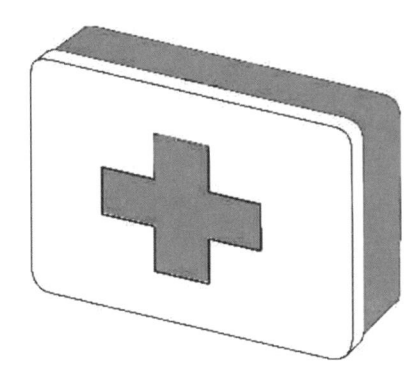

La Boulangerie

There is a bakery on every corner in France where a wide choice of bread is baked daily. The baker will often weigh the bread which is then sold according to weight .

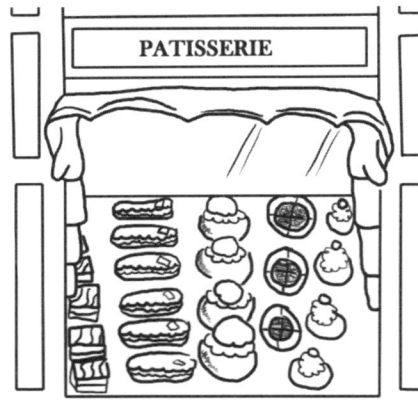

La Patisserie

There are almost as many shops selling cakes and pastries as there are bakeries and chemists in France. Sometimes La Patisserie sells chocolates and very often these are mac on the premises.

The tabac is a shop which opens early and where you can buy newspapers. Sometimes there are a number of tables where you very often see the older men sitting drinking strong black coffee and red wine.

Page 3
This page introduces the characters in the book as well as teaching your child how to introduce himself. The vocabulary section at the front of the book will help your child to understand the expressions. Help your child to look up these words in this section and then practice by asking him to find other words. Encourage your child to use these examples to learn how to say his name, then take on the role of other people, this will reinforce the expression 'je m'appelle'.

Page 4
It is very important to read the information box with your child, as it informs you on how to complete this workbook. The activity on this page provides practice writing French. Ensure that your child takes his time and encourage him to check his spelling using the vocabulary at the bottom of the page.

Page 5
This activity introduces the third person, 'Il' and 'Elle', 'He' and 'She'. Ask your child to find the name of each character, then introduce him as the third person. Encourage your child to use the vocabulary at the bottom of the page to look up how to say 'he/she is called' in French. Your child will then be able to write the characters' names in the space provided. Ask your child to repeat what he has written as this will reinforce this grammar point.

Page 6
This activity teaches your child shops in the town. Explain the significance of learning vocabulary, as it will be beneficial to your child if he ever goes to France. Encourage your child to use the vocabulary at the bottom of the page to complete the activity. Highlight the articles 'le' and 'la'. Explain that some words in French are masculine, some feminine and it is necessary to learn the article as well as the noun.

JE VAIS AU SUPERMARCHÉ ET J'ACHÉTE ...

juh vay o soo-per-mar-shay ay ja-shet
I go to the supermarket and I buy....

une limonade   un coca   - - - - - - - - - - - - - - - - -

- - - - - - - - - - - - - - -   - - - - - - - - - - - - - - -   du pain

un coca	un co-ca	coke
une limonade	oon lee-mon-ad	lemonade
du pain	do pan	bread
du lait	do lay	milk
des carottes	day car-rot	carrots
des oeufs	days erf	eggs
des bananes	day ban-nans	bananas
des petits pois	day petee pwa	peas

7
Sept

ELLE VA AU SUPERMARCHÉ ET ELLE ACHÉTE...

el va o soo-per-mar-shay ay el ashet
She goes to the supermarket and she buys...

du lait

des bananes   - - - - - - - - - - - - - - - - -   des carottes

8
Huit

Page 7

Ask your child to tell you how to do this exercise, as it is similar to the previous exercise. Highlight 'un' and 'une' and explain that they both mean 'a/one', then explain that 'un' is used with masculine nouns and 'une' for feminine nouns. When it comes to 'du', ask your child what we would say if we were buying bread and milk at a shop. We would say 'some milk and some bread'. That is why the French use 'du'. For plural nouns, the French use 'des' before the noun, after all we don't usually buy one carrot, one pea etc...!

Page 8

Always encourage your child to read the title on every page. Ask your child the difference between the title on page 7 and page 8. Although this activity continues to concentrate on the food vocabulary, this time we are talking about Sophie. Continue to encourage your child to check his spelling, using the vocabulary on page 7 and remember to praise your child's efforts.

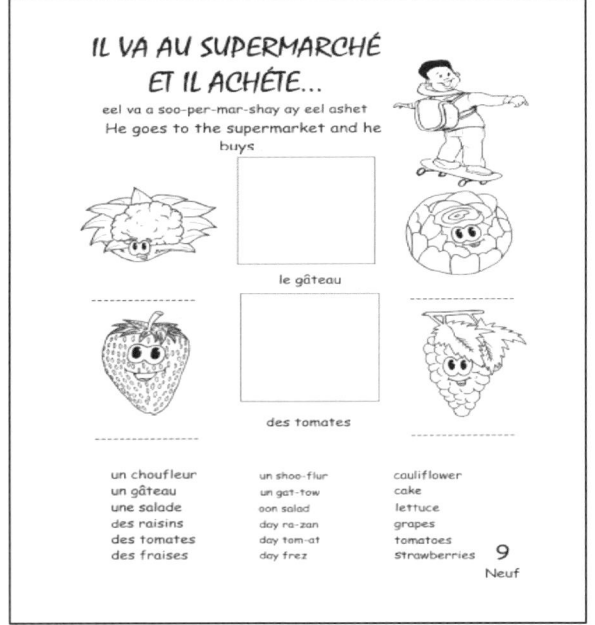

IL VA AU SUPERMARCHÉ ET IL ACHÉTE...

eel va a soo-per-mar-shay ay eel ashet
He goes to the supermarket and he buys

le gâteau

- - - - - - - - - - - - - - -   des tomates   - - - - - - - - - - - - - - -

un choufleur	un shoo-flur	cauliflower
un gâteau	un gat-tow	cake
une salade	oon salad	lettuce
des raisins	day ra-zan	grapes
des tomates	day tom-at	tomatoes
des fraises	day frez	strawberries

9
Neuf

TROUVE LES MOTS

W	E	R	G	H	H	J	E	G	A	M	O	R	F
D	G	S	J	K	A	P	P	L	O	U	E	D	G
A	B	A	N	A	N	E	E	A	F	H	E	P	F
H	J	N	K	K	R	G	T	C	H	I	P	S	S
G	W	D	R	Y	T	F	I	E	J	K	J	J	G
S	F	W	W	Q	M	N	T	I	K	X	C	Z	S
V	R	I	A	D	T	C	S	I	H	L	A	I	T
Z	C	C	V	N	M	O	P	K	H	F	R	I	O
R	T	H	A	F	G	C	O	Z	X	V	O	N	N
H	G	F	D	S	S	A	I	A	A	S	T	T	Y
L	J	H	P	A	I	N	S	L	O	Y	T	G	F
O	E	U	F	X	V	B	D	S	E	W	E	G	H
J	K	L	I	M	O	N	A	D	E	L	S	O	I
D	F	G	E	G	H	J	K	T	Y	R	E	D	B

See if you can help Patrice find these foods in the grid above...

BANANE	OEUF
COCA	CHIPS
SANDWICH	PETITS POIS
LIMONADE	FROMAGE
LAIT	CAROTTES
GLACE	PAIN

10
Dix

Page 9

Once again, ask you child to read the title on this page and ask him the name of the character in French, 'Il s'appelle Patrice'. Look at the vocabulary at the bottom of the page and ask your child to say what the French word is for each product, using the phonetics. Your child will then be able to complete the activity, always checking spellings.

Page 10

Before your child does the wordsearch, ask him to tell you what the words mean in English, then ask him where we would buy each item. For example, we would buy 'une glace' at 'le glacier'. If your child is not cooperating, leave this exercise and come back to it later. It is important that your child is enjoying what he is doing.

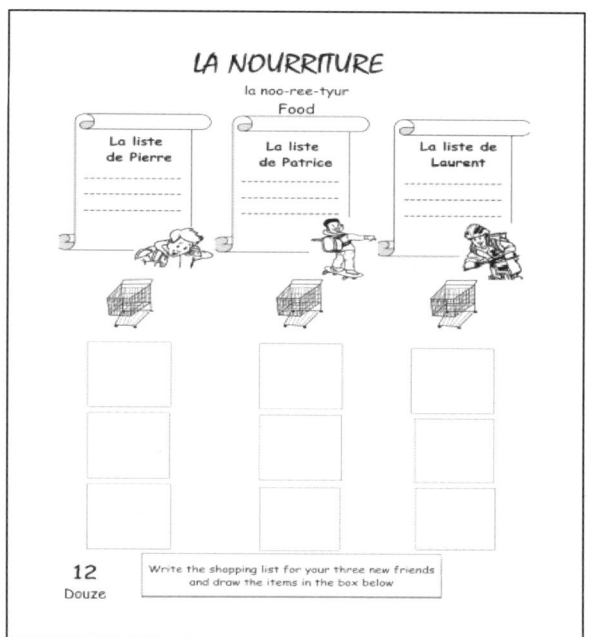

Page 11
Ask your child to read the shopping lists aloud in French before completing this exercise. If he is having problems with pronunciation, encourage your child to look back at the phonetics on the previous pages. You may wish to ask your child to write part of your shopping list in French, as this encourages your child to use French in a real situation.

Page 12
This activity allows your child to write his own shopping lists. Remember to remind him to check his spellings, using the vocabulary section at the front of the book or on the previous pages. Highlight the need to include the article, 'un, une, le, la, du, des'. Ask your child to read aloud his shopping lists in French.

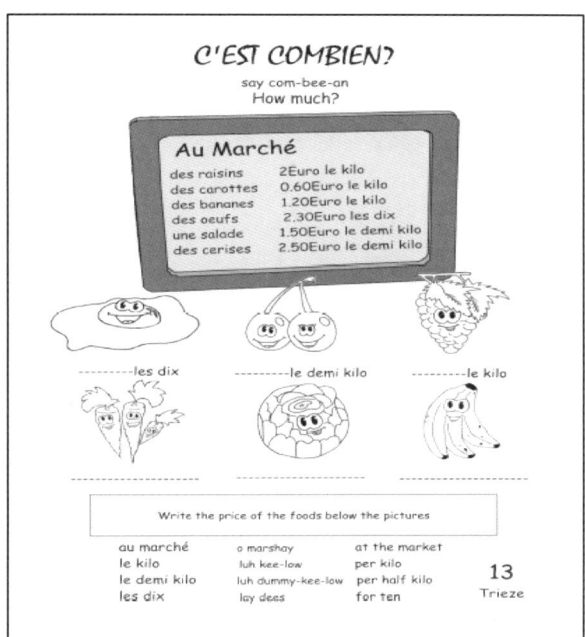

Page 13
This activity helps your child to understand that there are different currencies between countries and that currencies can change over time. Explain that other countries in Europe also have the Euro as their currency and that France only changed a few years ago from the Franc. The Euro is the equivalent to our pounds and the centime to our pence. This activity asks your child to write the price rather than the product. Highlight the vocabulary at the bottom of the page.

Page 14
This activity teaches your child how to ask for the products at the shop or market. Ask your child the question at the top of the page, 'Qu'est-ce que vous désirez?' and encourage your child to read aloud what the characters would like to buy. Refer to the phonetics at the bottom of the page. Your child can then write his own answer to the question, using the four examples as models.

Page 15
This page looks at some items that can be bought at the toy shop. Encourage your child to repeat the vocabulary, using the phonetics. If your child is confident using this vocabulary, encourage him to cover the words before tackling the activity. Remember to continue to praise your child's achievements.

Page 16
Ask your child to identify who is going to the toy shop. Encourage him to use full sentences, 'Elle s'appelle Sophie'. If your child is able to complete this exercise without looking at the previous page, encourage him to do so. It is vital that your child remembers the vocabulary that he has learnt throughout the book, so it is a good idea to continue to test him but in a fun way. When shopping, ask him what the items are in French. Ask him to find the item you say somewhere in the house (maybe hidden). Use as much French in the house as possible.

Page 17
Ask your child to tell you who is at the toy shop today and encourage him to use full sentences. This activity introduces your child to new vocabulary at the toy shop. Check your child's spelling and encourage him to take time and care over his work. Ask your child what he would buy at the toy shop. If possible, encourage him to use 'je voudrais' (I would like) before giving his answer.

Page 18
This wordsearch revises the vocabulary used in the previous pages. Therefore, try to encourage your child to understand what the words mean in English, before completing this activity. For extra work, your child could create his own wordsearch, using the vocabulary he has learnt so far in the book.

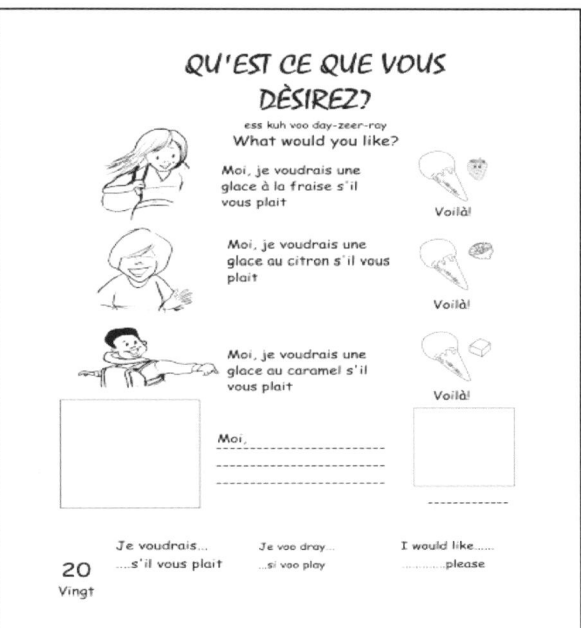

Page 19
Encourage your child to read the title of this page and ask him which shop he will be visiting and what item he will be buying. Take time to read the vocabulary at the bottom of the page and highlight the fact that in French the flavour of the ice cream comes after the noun, ice cream. Suggest to your child that he checks his spellings, using the vocabulary on the page.

Page 20
This page features three of the characters asking what they would like at the ice-cream parlour. Ask the question at the top of the page and encourage your child to say what each character would like in French. Your child can then write what he would ask for at the ice-cream parlour. Highlight that your child has already learnt 'je voudrais' earlier in the book and discuss how often this one phrase can be used. This helps your child to understand that certain words and phrases can be used in different situations.

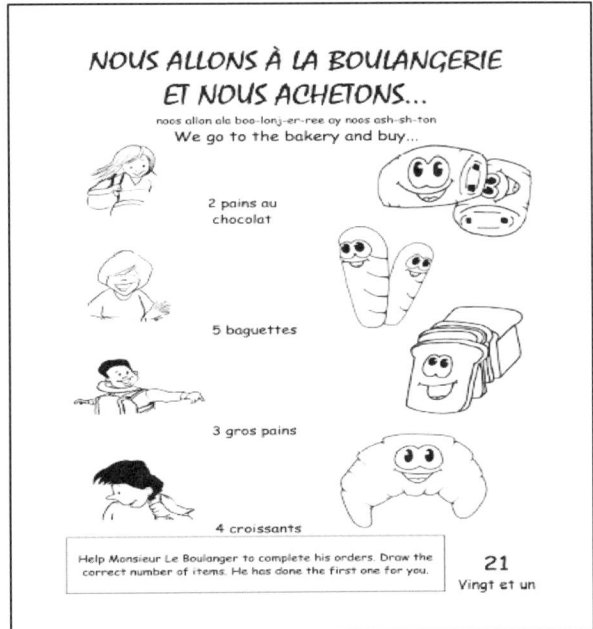

Page 21
This activity introduces the second person plural 'nous' (we). This is the last personal pronoun that your child will be introduced to in this workbook. Talk about the title of the page and emphasise the fact that we are now talking about 'we' and ask your child which shop we are visiting. Help your child with the vocabulary on this page and try to count to 10 or more in French with your child. The numbers in French are at the bottom of each page.

Page 22

Talk about the title of the page with your child and ask him to tell you which shop we are visiting. Remind your child to read the vocabulary at the bottom of the page before rushing on to the next page. Emphasise the importance of both learning how to spell and how to say new vocabulary.

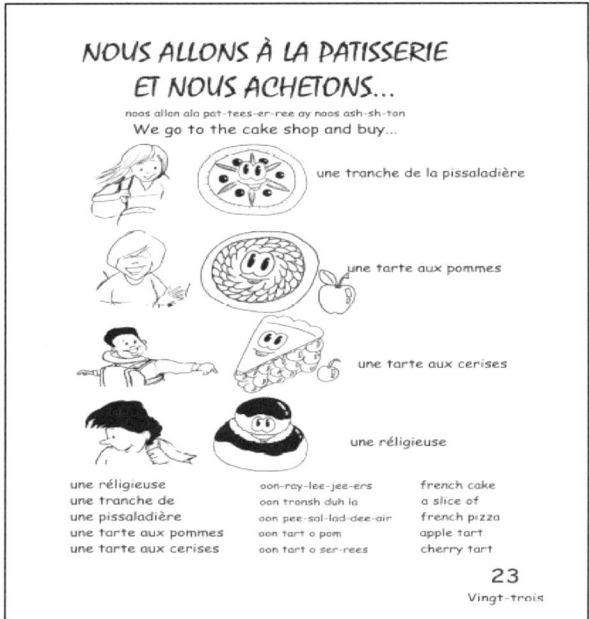

NOUS ALLONS À LA PATISSERIE ET NOUS ACHETONS...

noos allon ala pat-tees-er-ree ay noos ash-sh-ton
We go to the cake shop and buy...

une tranche de la pissaladière

une tarte aux pommes

une tarte aux cerises

une réligieuse

une réligieuse	oon-ray-lee-jee-ers	french cake
une tranche de une pissaladière	oon tronsh duh la oon pee-sal-lad-dee-air	a slice of french pizza
une tarte aux pommes	oon tart o pom	apple tart
une tarte aux cerises	oon tart o ser-rees	cherry tart

23
Vingt-trois

Page 23
Introduce your child to the vocabulary at the bottom of the page before completing the exercise. As an extra, find the items on the page around the house and put them on the table. Ask your child to name the items in French. Then take one away and ask what is missing. Many children enjoy playing games like these as it helps them learn vocabulary as well as having fun. Award 'the cake shop' sticker.

ELLE VA AU TABAC ET ELLE ACHETE...

el va o tab-bac ay el ashet
She goes to the newsagents and buys...

des bonbons

un cahier

une carte postale

un crayon	un cray-yon	pencil
un journal	un joor-nal	newspaper
un cahier	un cai-yay	exercise book
une timbre	oon tam-bra	stamp
une carte postale	oon cart post-tal	postcard
des bonbons	day bon-bon	sweets

24
Vingt-Quatre

Page 24
On this page, your child learns vocabulary of items found at the Tabac. Encourage your child to say these items aloud a few times before completing the exercise. Emphasise the need to take time over work and always to check spellings. Award the 'newsagents' sticker.

JE VAIS À LA PHARMACIE ET J'ACHÈTE...

je vay ala far-mass-see ay jashet
I go to the chemist and I buy...

des couches

le gel douche

une brosse à cheveux

le maquillage

une brosse à dents	oon bross a don	toothbrush
une brosse à cheveux	oon bross a sh-vuh	hairbrush
le parfum	luh par-fam	perfume
le maquillage	luh mac-key-aj	make-up
le gel douche	luh jel doosh	showergel
des couches	day coosh	nappies

25
Vingt-cinq

Page 25
This page looks at some items that can be bought at the chemist. Encourage your child to repeat the vocabulary using the phonetics. Again, once he knows this vocabulary, encourage him to cover the English translation and then give the name of the word in english.

JE VAIS À LA PHARMACIE ET J'ACHÈTE...

je vay ala far-mass-see ay jashet
I go to the chemist and I buy...

le shampooing

des pastilles

le poudre

le rouge à lèvres

le shampooing	luh shampooing	shampoo
le poudre de talc	luh poo-dra duh talc	talcum powder
le rouge à lèvres	luh rooj a levra	lipstick
des comprimès	day com-pree-may	tablets
le dentifrice	luh don-tee-freese	toothpaste
des pastilles	day pas-teel	cough drops

26
Vingt-six

Page 25
The French word 'pharmacie' is like the English word 'pharmacist' with which your child might be familiar. Draw his attention to the fact that many of the French words for shops end in -ie. List the shops on a piece of paper that end in -ie and draw a picture of what you can buy at each one along-side.

Page 27
Ask your child to tell you who is at the chemist today and again encourage him to use a full sentence - We have practised this sentence before, so he will be familiar with the sentence. Check your child's spelling and praise his efforts. This new vocabulary is quite difficult so try and make your child aware of the progress he has made.

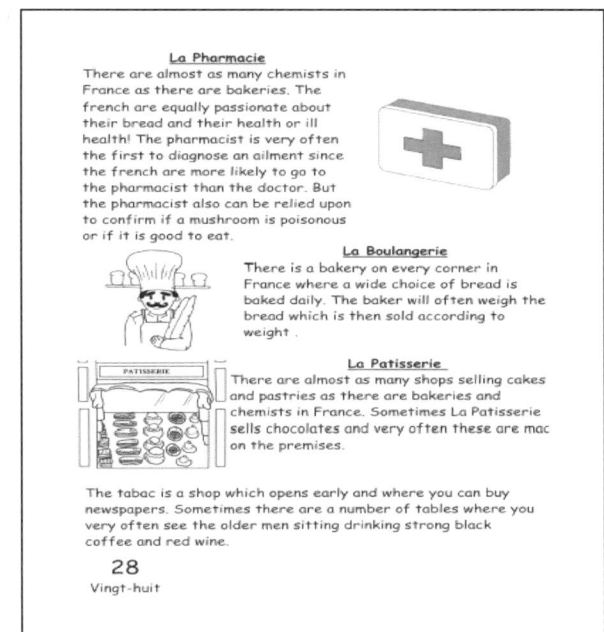

Page 28
This page details the significance of 'La Pharmacie - the chemist', 'La Boulangerie - the bakery', 'La patisserie - the cake shop' and 'Le Tabac - the newsagents' in French life. Perhaps your child would enjoy 'building' a French town, 'Frogs Legs for Tea' - will show you how this can be easily achieved!

VOCABULARY LIST

French	Phonetics	English
un avion	un av-vee-on	aeroplane
une baguette	oon bag-ett	stick of bread
un ballon	un bal-lon	ball
des bananes	day ban-nan	bananas
un bateau	un bat-tow	boat
des bonbons	day bon-bon	sweets
la boulangerie	la boo-lonj-er-ree	bakers
une brosse à cheveux	oon bross a sh-vuh	hairbrush
une brosse à dents	oon bross a don	toothbrush
un cahier	un cai-yay	exercise book
des carottes	day car-rot	carrots
une carte postale	oon cart post-tal	postcard
un cerf volant	un sef-vol-lon	kite
le choufleur	luh shoo-flur	cauliflower
un coca	un co-ca	coke
des couches	day coosh	nappies
un crayon	un cray-yon	pencil
des crayons	day cray-yons	crayons
des croissants	day kwa-son	croissants
les dix	lay dees	for ten
des fraises	day frez	strawberries

VOCABULARY LIST CONTINUED

French	Phonetics	English
le gâteau	luh gat-tow	cake
le gel douche	luh jel doosh	showergel
une glace à la fraise	oon glass a la frez	strawberry ice cream
une glace à la vanille	oon glass a la vanee	vanilla ice cream
une glace au caramel	oon glass oh cara mel	caramel ice cream
une glace au chocolat	oon glass oh shoc-o-lat	chocolate ice cream
une glace au citron	oon glass oh seetron	lemon ice cream
une glace au melon	oon glass oh meh-lon	melon ice cream
le glacier	luh glass-see-ay	ice-cream parlour
un gros pain	un gro pan	bread (large)
un journal	un joor-nal	newspaper
du lait	do lay	milk
le demi kilo	luh demmy-kee-low	per half kilo
le kilo	luh kee-low	per kilo
une limonade	oon lee-mon-ad	lemonade
un livre	un livra	book
le magasin de jouets	luh maga-zan duh joo-ay	toy shop
le maquillage	luh mac-key-aj	make-up
le marché	luh marshay	market
au marché	o marshay	at the market
la nourriture	la noo-ree-tyur	food
un nounours	un noo-noors	teddy
des oeufs	days erf	eggs
du pain	do pan	bread
un pain au chocolat	do pan	chocolate bread
une parapluie	oon para-plwee	umbrella
le parfum	luh par-fam	perfume
la pâtisserie	la pat-tees-er-ee	cake shop
des petits pois	day petee pwa	peas
la pharmacie	la far-mass-see	chemist
des raisins	day ra-zan	grapes
une réligieuse	oon-ray-lee-jee-ers	french cake
la salade	la salad	lettuce
un skate	un skate	skateboard
un stylo	un stee-lo	pen
le supermarché	luh soo-per-mar-shay	supermarket
le tabac	luh tab-bac	newsagents
un tambour	un tom-boor	drum
une tarte aux cerises	oon tart o ser-rees	cherry tart
une tarte aux pommes	oon tart o pom	apple tart
une timbre	oon tam-bra	stamp
des tomates	day tom-at	tomatoes
un train	un tran	train
la pissaladière	la pee-sal-lad-dee-air	french pizza
un vélo	un vay-lo	bike
une voiture	oon vwat-tyor	car